I0159576

WHAT YOU HAVE IS ENOUGH TO GET STARTED

by Norman H. Lyons, Jr.

WHAT YOU HAVE
IS ENOUGH TO GET STARTED

by Norman H. Lyons, Jr.

NVP

NUVISION PUBLISHING

Copyright © 2021 Norman H. Lyons, Jr.
All rights reserved.

No part of this book may be used
or reproduced by any means, graphic, electronic,
or mechanical, including photocopying, recording,
taping or by any information storage retrieval system
without the written permission of
the author except in the case of brief quotations
embodied in critical articles and reviews.

Scriptures references are taken from the
KING JAMES VERSION (KJV),
public domain unless otherwise notated.
All rights reserved.

Books may be ordered through booksellers
or by contacting:
normanlyonsjrministries.com
Norman H. Lyons, Jr.
PO Box 86
Uniondale NY 11553

ISBN# 978-1-5136-8863-3

NUVISION PUBLISHING
PO Box 4455 | Wilmington NC
www.nuvisiondesigns.biz

Printed in the United States of America.

After Mary McLeod Bethune had endured the pain and overcame the barriers to educate herself, she applied to various schools to be employed as a teacher. After being consistently denied because of her race, she decided to start her own school.

Then she took a leap of faith and did something absolutely incredible. She went out into the woods and began to pick berries. After picking a sufficient amount of berries, she commenced to bleed the berries and make ink. Mary made her own ink, and then started her own school, so she could fulfill her dream of becoming a teacher. This is a classic example of understanding that **What You Have is Enough to Get Started.**

So often we are overcome by the reality of what we don't have. In life there will always be something that eludes us even if only temporarily. Therefore, we should never be so intimidated by what we do not possess to the extent we neglect to use what we do have. When you begin to utilize and take advantage of your resources, you will eventually obtain what you didn't have originally. A wise man states this truth another way: "What you've got will produce what you've not." Mary McLeod Bethune didn't have the standard resources to start a school available to her but she did have access to clusters of berries growing in the woods. Instead of opining about what she did not have, she went out into the woods and made use of what she did have. The time has come for us to begin to use what we **do have** in order to produce what we **don't have.**

Throughout the scriptures God takes the little that is originally available and makes it work towards great accomplishments. From the rib bone of man, he made woman. With a shepherd boy he destroyed a giant. With a single rod he parted waves of water. God has perfected the use of one to put a thousand to flight. This is the nature of the God we serve. We can never determine what he will do based only on what we see available.

"And Jonathan said to the young man that bare his armor, come, and let us go over unto the garrison of these uncircumcised: it may be that the Lord will work for us: for there is no restraint to the Lord to save by

many or by few." (I Samuel 14:6)

There is "no restraint to the Lord..." This truth is overwhelming when we contemplate its ramifications. In essence, Jonathan was operating according to the understanding that God is the essence of unlimited ability. Serving God avails us to an unrestricted resource. God's power is not limited by human lack, flack or set back. We must meditate on the reality of God's ability.

"And now unto Him, who is able to do exceeding, abundantly, above all you can ask or think according to the power that worketh in us." (Ephesians 3:20)

We could learn a thing or two from the little boy who was about three feet tall but found a way to get on top of our one-story building. He inadvertently threw his ball on the roof of our church. Without a ladder, height, or a friend's help, he managed to scale our building. Hearing footsteps running over my office where I was writing this booklet, I ran out to see who was trespassing on church property. To my surprise this short young lad came down the side of our building.

After advising him of the hazards of such endeavors, I asked him how he managed to get up so high, being so small? He showed me how he straddled the parking lot cable barrier to get to the mini-bus parked alongside the church building. From the front side of the mini-bus he grabbed the antennae brackets and pulled himself up to the bus top. From the top of the bus, he leaped to the side of the roof and pulled himself up onto the roof top. I thought that was a lot to go through to retrieve a ball. But apparently it meant enough to him to warrant the struggle. The question is, do our goals mean enough to warrant the struggle? When your goals are significant, your mind and heart should be engaged to achieve them. Reverend Jesse Jackson said, "If your mind can conceive it, and your heart can believe it, you can achieve it." And Jesus said, *"...nothing shall be impossible to him that believes."*

I want you to believe in God, believe in yourself and believe that what you already have is enough to get started! You can have ability. You can have tools and equipment. You can have an opportunity. However, if you don't believe in the potential of your immediate supply, you won't take action.

The Bible contains examples of individuals who had little to start with but commenced anyway. It is my conviction that Biblical examples are the best examples. Therefore, let us review a scriptural success story that proves little can accomplish a lot if you dare to get started.

Moses had a great mission but initially he underestimated his God, himself, and his resources. Moses had some serious questions. His first question was: *"Who am I?" (Exodus 3:11)* Moses questioned his own ability to be even identified with such a great ministry of deliverance. Pay attention to the response he received from God:

"And He said, certainly I will be with thee, and this shall be a token unto thee; that I have sent thee: when thou hast brought

forth the people out of Egypt, ye shall serve God upon this mountain." (Exodus 3:12)

Note how the token was going to be an afterward reality. This demanded faith from Moses to step out on God's Word and get started. Sometimes we look for a sign when we ought to be listening for a Word.

A spoken Word of God unseen is better than a sign that is seen.

God was training Moses to hear and heed his voice regardless of what he didn't see. If we can learn to use God's Word and get started no matter what we don't see, we will eventually live to see something worthwhile.

Moses' first question was concerning himself; his second question was concerning the people.

"And Moses said unto God, Behold, when I come unto the children of Israel, and shall say unto them, the God of your Fathers hath sent me unto you; and they shall say to me, what is his name? What shall I say unto them?" (Exodus 3:13)

Sometimes we do not act on callings and ideas because of ourselves, and at other times, we allow people and their questions to stifle us. After God addressed Moses' personal problem, God then responded to the people's problem. If you will allow God to deal with you, he will tell and teach you how to deal with people. From Exodus 3:14 through 3:18, God tells Moses what to say to the people. Therein is a key to dealing with people in light of your destiny. Tell them only what God is saying to them and not what God is saying to you. Tell yourself what God tells you and not the people. Tell the people what God is saying to them. Remember to take the time to know the difference. If you allow them, people will disconnect you from your destiny. Do not allow them.

Moses' third problem was a people problem as well. He was concerned about what "...they will say..." more than what God has said. Moses feared public opinion.

"And Moses answered and said, but behold they will not believe me, nor hearken unto my voice: for they will say, the Lord hath not appeared unto thee." (Exodus 4:1)

Like many of us, Moses wanted to be liked by the people. He liked being understood by the people. He liked being

14

reaffirmed by the people.

We must realize that the pleasures of the people are potentially as poisonous as the pleasures of sin.

They both only last for a season.

When we accept this reality, we will be more attracted to the presence of God. As we cultivate the discipline of entering into his presence, we will find true and lasting pleasure.

"Thou wilt shew me the path of life: in thy presence is fullness of joy; at thy right hand there are pleasures for evermore." (Psalm 16:11)

Every person who is serious about getting on the road to their divine destiny, **must decide to prefer the presence of God over the presence of people.**

God answered Moses by question and by wonders. His question was: "What is that in thine hand?" Never mind about the people. Never mind their faithlessness. Never mind what they will say. Never mind what you do not have. Never mind what is not there. Tell me what you do have because that is what you must use to get past all the blockades and barriers. In other words, God was saying to Moses, stop taking inventory of things that are not there. Start taking inventory of what is there. Stop crying over the unavailable and start magnifying that which is available. Stop telling me about the things that are not and start telling me what you have got.

"WHAT IS IN THINE HAND?"

This is the question we must ask and answer in our own lives in order to successfully get started. What do I have? What has God given me to work with? What are my strengths? What are my gifts? What do I have at hand? These questions cry out for introspective investigation. They demand that we concentrate until we come to some concise conclusions. I will call this type of research **"in-house homework"**.

When you complete your **"in-house homework"** assignment, you can tell God what you have. Once you know what you have to the extent you are confident to tell

God you have it, he will tell you how to use it.

"And the Lord said unto him, what is that in thine hand? And he said, a rod. [3] And he said, cast it on the ground. And he cast it on the ground, and it became a serpent; and Moses fled from before it. [4] And the Lord said unto Moses, put forth thine hand, and take it by the tail. And he put forth his hand, and caught it, and it became a rod in his hand: [5] That they may believe that the Lord God of their Fathers, The God of Abraham, the God of Isaac, and the God of Jacob, hath appeared unto thee." (Exodus 4:2-5)

God showed Moses the magnitude of what he had and how it worked within his divine destiny. God knows what he put in us;

we are the ones who have to find it out. God asked Moses, "What is that…" not because he did not know, but because he wanted Moses to concentrate on what was in his hand instead of what was out of reach. It was a question that caused him to redirect his attention. God already knew what "that" was and how he was going to use it. That rod in hand would be a divine weapon against the scepter of Pharoah.

Moses was sent to do spiritual battle with the earthly ruler of the known world. Even though God was sending him without an army he was not sending him empty-handed. God showed Moses his rod and how it worked. He explained its significance and impact upon his mission.

Likewise, we must allow God to show

us how our gifts work for his glory. We need an understanding of how what we have fits into God's plan for our life.

"Wisdom is the principal thing, therefore get wisdom: and with all thy getting get understanding." (Proverbs 4:7)

TAKE YOUR STICK AND SHOW SOME SIGNS

Being endowed with resources and ability is not enough; we need to know how to use what we have. Since every good and perfect gift comes from above (James 1:17), we ought to allow God to show us how to use what he gave us. Regardless of how useful Moses' rod was prior to his call, it was transformed into a miraculous weapon after his call. That rod had been there all the time, but its significance laid dormant until God separated it and sanctified it unto His purpose. This is the type of transformation and understanding we need to see and experience in our lives. **We need to know**

23

what we have and how it works within God's overall plan for our life.

Moses' final excuse was his inability and inexperience. Maybe he doubted that the people would believe because he really did not believe. Moses' personal problem was that he did not know that God sends people that cannot go without Him. Moses did not know that he did not have to have ability and experience. Moses did not know that God was his ability and experience. Moses did not know that all he needed to be was obedient. Moses did not know that once you know the will of God for your life, all you have to do is get started.

"And Moses said unto the Lord, O My Lord, I am not eloquent, neither heretofore, nor since thou hast spoken unto thy servant:

but I am slow of speech, and of slow tongue."
(Exodus 4:10)

Moses was afraid of what he knew and afraid of what he did not know. Moses knew he was not articulate; he knew he was not an orator, and that made him fearful. Moses did not have any experience in being a prophet. He said God had never dealt with him in this manner. This prophetic, miraculous, deliverance ministry stuff was a whole new world. This made him fearful.

Do you know what your fears are? Have you ever told God about your fears? This was the best time for fear to be dealt with. Before you embark, before you get started; make up your mind to start fear-free. Get free then start. Fear is horrible because it is the expectation of negative results. It is the opposite of faith. **Fear turns the devil on like faith turns God on.** Therefore, starve your fear to death. Do not just put it on a diet but starve that spirit to death. Ask God to supernaturally remove it and start resisting it yourself. As God hits it high, you hit it low.

You bind it below and God will bind it above.

When Moses confessed his feelings to God, he exposed the internal stronghold. Fear of inability and inexperience was the stronghold. Even though it angered God that Moses was yet fearful, God yet addressed the problem. An angry God on your side is better than the devil's lies locked inside. Fear is actually the devil's lies locked inside you. When you call out to God, he will help you.

"And call upon me in the day of trouble: I will deliver thee, and thou shalt glorify me." (Psalm 50:15)

"And the Lord said unto him, who hath made man's mouth? Or who maketh the dumb, or deaf, or the seeing, or the blind? Have not I the Lord? [12] Now therefore go, and I will be with thy mouth, and teach thee what thou shalt say. [13] And he said, O my Lord, send, I pray thee, by the hand of him whom thou wilt send. [14] And the anger of the Lord was kindled against Moses, and he said, Is not Aaron the Levite thy brother? I know that he can speak well. And also, behold, he cometh forth to meet thee: and when he seeth thee, he will be glad in heart. [15] And thou shalt speak unto him, and put words in his mouth: and I will be with thy mouth, and with his mouth, and will teach you what ye shall do. [16] And he shall be thy spokeman unto the people: And he shall be, even he shall be to thee instead of a mouth, and thou shalt be to him instead of God." (Exodus 4:11-16)

Once again God asked Moses questions that forced him to redirect his thinking. God reminded Moses that he is the creator (Exodus 4:11). He commanded Moses to go and know that he would be his speech therapist (Exodus 4:12). In other words, get started because you have me. We need to be reminded of the ability of God. It is not that we never found out, we just forgot. We forgot who made the morning stars sing together and the sons of God shout for joy. Sometimes the intimidating circumstances of our existence cause us to forget. We simply stop thinking about the vastness of God. Yet in all of this God has a question that rekindles your remembrance.

"Hast thou not known? Hast thou not heard, that the everlasting God, the Lord, the Creator of the ends of the earth, fainteth not, neither is weary? There is no searching of his understanding." (Isaiah 40:28)

Having all his excuses overruled, Moses makes his desperate plea for God to send someone else (Exodus 4:14). But God sent Aaron with him, not to replace him. **Sometimes we seek to be replaced when all we need is divinely sent assistance.** Aaron was to be the spokesman, but Moses was to receive the Word from the Lord. God's final word to Moses before he actually got started was:

"And thou shalt take this rod in thine hand, where with thou shalt do signs."

This is the place where God wants all his servants to come. We should come to the realization that it is time to get started. Realize the night is far spent. Realize the Kingdom of God is at hand. Realize we ought not to be slothful. Realize tomorrow is coming but today is already here. Realize a rod in hand is better than anything else that is on the way. So, I say to you, take your stick and show some signs because **what you have is enough to get started.**

"And Moses went and returned to Jethro his Father in law, and said unto him,

let me go, I pray thee, and return unto my brethren which are in Egypt, and see whether they be yet alive. And Jethro said to Moses, go in peace." (Exodus 4:18)

Moses went on to be God's agent to deliver Israel from Egyptian bondage. God gave him miraculous signs and wonders wrought by his rod to break the back of slavery over his people. That glorious journey began with Moses having to come to grips with the fact that what he had, be it ever so humble, was enough to get started.

CONCLUSION

There was a pastor that was despondent over the lack of resources to fulfill his vision for the church. One night he went to sleep and had a revelatory dream. In the dream he was standing side by side with a group of preachers. Every preacher had a shovel except for him. He was given a small silver spoon. He complained about the unfairness of being given a small silver spoon when the other preachers were given a shovel. Then the Lord told all the preachers to start digging. The preacher with the spoon continued to complain and argue with the Lord about his unfair disadvantage. To this the Lord just said, "Stick your spoon in the ground."

The preacher kept reiterating his complaint of unfairness and the Lord's response remained the same, "Stick your spoon in the ground." Finally, while still complaining, the preacher stuck his spoon in the ground. When his spoon touched the surface of the earth, miraculously the ground opened up into a huge hole for a foundation to be built.

What the preacher thought was an unfair disadvantage, was an unfair advantage of favor bestowed upon him in disguise. Oh, what a blessing he would have forfeited if he had not stuck his spoon into the ground.

My friends never fail to use whatever God has given you to get started. Don't complain, don't hesitate and compare yourself to others. Get on with the business of making full proof of your ministry and make use of your gifts. Put your little spoon in the ground and watch God make a way out of no way for you. Always remember,

<u>What You Have Is Enough to Get Started</u>.

THE ABC'S OF SALVATION

1. Admit that you have sinned. "For all have sinned, and come short of the glory of God." (Romans 3:23)

2. Believe on Jesus Christ the Savior. "For God so loved the world, that he gave his only begotten Son, that whosoever Believeth in Him should not perish, but have everlasting life." (John 3:16)

3. Confess. "That if thou shalt confess with thy mouth the Lord Jesus and shalt believe in thine heart that God hath raised him from the dead, thou shalt be saved, For with the heart man believeth unto righteousness; and with the mouth

confession is made unto salvation."
(Romans 10: 9-10)

A PRAYER FOR SALVATION

"Heavenly Father in Jesus name, I confess that I am a sinner. Forgive me for my sin and save me. I repent of my sin. I believe in my heart on the Lord Jesus Christ and confess with my mouth that I accept Him as my personal Lord and Saviour. Thank you for saving me. Amen."

BIOGRAPHICAL SKETCH
OF THE AUTHOR

Bishop Norman Lyons, Jr. is the founder and senior pastor of the Fountain of Life Church in Uniondale, New York. Bishop Lyons was born and raised in the Church of God in Christ. He benefited from the disciplines of the Church and excelled in his ministerial training. As a result, he was ordained by Bishop O. M. Kelly who was his highest-ranking spiritual patriarch.

In addition to his national ministry, he has also done missionary work in Haiti, Nigeria, West Africa and Italy. Bishop Lyons has served as an executive council member of the International Council of Local

Churches. He has also served as a member of M.E.C.C.A. For seven years Bishop Lyons was a Board Member of the New York Call hosted by Pastor Donnie McClurkin. Bishop Lyons is Chaplain Emeritus for the Long Island Conference of Clergy.

At the time of this writing, Bishop Lyons has been preaching for 42 years. He has been married to his darling wife, Pastor Sharon, for 41 years. They have pastored the Fountain of Life Church for 38 years.

Norman and Sharon are the grateful parents of two daughters, Juliet and Jasmine. They also have been blessed with a son-in-love, Joaquin, Juliet's husband.

www.ingramcontent.com/pod-product-compliance
Lightning Source LLC
Chambersburg PA
CBHW060633030426
42337CB00018B/3332